BACK FROM
THE BRINK

12 AMPHIBIANS
BACK FROM THE BRINK

by Samantha S. Bell

12 STORY
LIBRARY

www.12StoryLibrary.com

12-Story Library is an imprint of Peterson Publishing Company and Press Room Editions.

Produced for 12-Story Library by Red Line Editorial

Photographs ©: Doug Lemke/Shutterstock Images, cover, 1; Dror Galili/AP Images, 4, 28; Pan Xunbin/Shutterstock Images, 6; Julie Larsen Maheri/Wildlife Conservation Society/AP Images, 7; Darren Green/Shutterstock Images, 8; Cynthia Kidwell/Shutterstock Images, 9; Lefteris Papaulakis/Shutterstock Images, 10; Mark Baker/AP Images, 11; David W. Leindecker/Shutterstock Images, 13, 29; John Measey, 14, 15; TopPhoto/AP Images, 16; Chesapeake Images/Shutterstock Images, 18; Bruce MacQueen/Shutterstock Images, 19; Animals Animals/SuperStock, 21; Eric Gay/AP Images, 23; Perth Zoo, 24; Tom Grundy/Shutterstock Images, 26; Jason Mintzer/Shutterstock Images, 27

ISBN
978-1-63235-000-8 (hardcover)
978-1-63235-060-2 (paperback)
978-1-62143-041-4 (hosted ebook)

Library of Congress Control Number: 2014937243

Printed in the United States of America
Mankato, MN
June, 2014

Go beyond the book. Get free, up-to-date content on this topic at 12StoryLibrary.com.

TABLE OF CONTENTS

HULA PAINTED FROG NOT EXTINCT AFTER ALL

A black belly and white spots make the Hula painted frog easy to recognize. The first two frogs were discovered in 1940 near Israel's Hula Lake. Another one was found in 1955. Then the lake and wetlands were drained to help stop the spread of malaria, a disease carried by mosquitoes. No one saw the frogs for decades after that. Scientists thought they were extinct.

Years later, the lake was turned into a nature reserve. The area could

The Hula painted frog has a black underside with white dots.

IUCN RED LIST

The International Union for the Conservation of Nature (IUCN) keeps a list of all threatened species in the world, called the Red List. Each species is labeled according to how at risk it is.

Least Concern: Not considered at risk.

Near Threatened: At risk of being vulnerable or endangered in the future.

Vulnerable: At risk of extinction.

Endangered: At high risk of extinction.

Critically Endangered: At extremely high risk of extinction.

Extinct in the Wild: Only lives in captivity.

Extinct: No members of a species are left.

support wildlife again. Then in 2011, a park ranger was on patrol. A Hula painted frog jumped right in front of him.

Since then, approximately 14 Hula painted frogs have been found. The population seems to be small, but the state of the frogs' habitat is promising. The lake is cleaner than before, and a deadly fungus that has killed other frogs around the world is nowhere to be seen. Since the Hula painted frog has only recently been rediscovered, Israel has just started plans for its conservation.

Scientists have another reason to be excited about the rediscovery of this frog. They have determined the Hula painted frog belongs to a particular group of amphibians that they thought was long gone. Before this discovery, scientists could only study this amphibian group, *Latonia*, through fossils.

0

Number of Hula painted frogs spotted between 1955 and 2011.

Status: Critically endangered
Population: Unknown
Home: Israel
Life Span: Unknown

HELLBENDER SALAMANDERS HEAD BACK TO STREAMS

Devil dog, lasagna lizard, and snot otter are some of the hellbender salamander's nicknames. Found in cold mountain streams, these salamanders can grow up to two feet (0.6 m) long. Their dark coloring helps them to blend in with river rocks or driftwood. In recent years, the salamanders became even harder to find.

Hellbender salamanders can only survive in a very specific habitat. They breathe underwater through pores in their skin. They have to live in flowing streams to do this. If the water flow is too slow, not enough water will pass over the salamander. It will not get enough oxygen. Man-made dams have decreased water flow.

The hellbenders have other problems, too. Erosion has covered rocks that they use for nesting. And construction and agriculture activities have polluted the water in some areas. Sometimes fishermen kill the salamanders because they think they are poisonous, even though they are not. Natural predators also eat the salamanders' young. Since the 1980s, hellbender

Hellbenders use their strong sense of smell to detect food, such as worms and small fish.

Hellbenders are the world's third-largest species of salamander.

populations in some areas had decreased by almost half.

Some groups have worked to repair hellbenders' habitats. They replaced flat rocks in the streams for the salamanders to use for nesting. Scientists also found that not enough young hellbenders seemed to be making it to adulthood in the wild. So they started raising them in captivity. They released the salamanders once they were at least 12 inches (30.5 cm) long. At that size, they were big enough to avoid most predators. Hundreds of hellbender salamanders have been reintroduced into the wild in this way.

160 million

Years the hellbender has been around, according to fossil records.

Status: Near threatened
Population: Unknown
Home: United States
Life Span: 30 years

THINK ABOUT IT

When amphibians are not doing well, it is often an indicator of poor water quality. Pollution, erosion, and dams can all affect water quality. When these problems occur, how do you think other animals are affected?

PANAMANIAN GOLDEN FROG SAVED FROM CLOSE CALL

The spots on Panamanian golden frogs make each one unique. No two patterns are exactly alike. But the golden frogs all face the same deadly disease. A fungus called Chytrid is attacking their skin. A frog's thin, moist skin helps it to breathe. When the fungus covers the skin, the frog can't take in enough oxygen.

The same disease had already wiped out other amphibians in Central America and other parts of the world. A biologist first found an infected golden frog in 2006. He knew he had to act quickly to save the species. Soon scientists, zoo employees, and other volunteers started flying in to help. Volunteers collected healthy golden frogs and

Golden frogs release a poison through their skin to keep predators away.

8

Golden frogs used to live near streams in the Panamanian rain forest.

other amphibians. Then they set up a temporary home for them in a local hotel. The frogs were given clean cages and fed live insects. There they were safe from infection.

The frogs lived at the hotel while new homes could be arranged. The Houston Zoo in Texas set up a habitat for them. So did a zoo in Panama. The golden frogs have not been seen in the wild since 2009. But they are thriving in captivity. In this case, the quick efforts of a few seem to have saved this

species from extinction. Scientists hope to figure out someday how to protect the frogs from the fungus so that they can return to the wild.

200–600

Number of eggs a single egg clutch might hold.

Status: Critically endangered
Population: Unknown
Home: Panama
Life Span: Five years

TREASURED SYMBOL

Golden frogs have been a national symbol for luck in Panama since ancient Mayan times. Some people still believe that seeing a golden frog will bring good fortune. The frog's image is featured on Panamanian lottery tickets.

SOUTHERN CORROBOREE FROG SAVED FROM DEADLY FUNGUS

Most poisonous frogs pick up chemicals from the insects they eat. But southern corroboree frogs make their own poison. They release it through their skin. Their bright yellow stripes warn predators to stay away. These tiny frogs measure approximately 1 inch (2.5 cm) long. Until the 1970s, they were seen in large numbers high up in the snowy mountains of Australia.

Southern corroboree frogs lay eggs on land instead of in water like most amphibians. In the fall, heavy rains flood the nest and the eggs hatch. Young frogs called tadpoles also need water to swim in. Too many years of drought meant few tadpoles were surviving to adulthood. In the 1970s, the deadly Chytrid fungus

The southern corroboree frog was featured on an Australian stamp to raise awareness.

Corroboree Frog

AUSTRALIA 3c

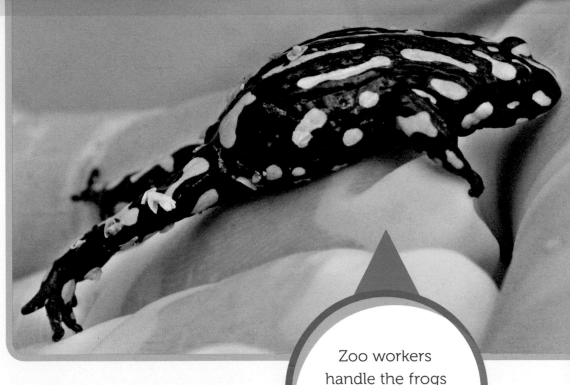

was found in Australia. The fungus spread quickly from frog to frog. The corroboree frogs' numbers soon fell to fewer than 100 in the wild.

In 2001, zoo workers started collecting eggs and hatching them in captivity. The frogs are kept in refrigerated habitats because they are used to the cold. Scientists have been exposing them to the fungus. With exposure over time, the frogs' bodies may become able to fight off the disease. Scientists hope to breed large numbers of the frogs so that they can be released again in the wild someday.

Zoo workers handle the frogs carefully because of their poisonous skin.

4,265
Distance in feet (1,300 m) above sea level where southern corroboree frogs live.

Status: Critically endangered
Population: Fewer than 100
Home: Australia
Life Span: Nine years

5

TINY KIHANSI SPRAY TOADS MAKE BIG RETURN

The Kihansi spray toad gives birth to tiny, fully formed babies. One baby toad can fit on the head of a pin. Fully grown, the toads are only approximately 1.1 inches (2.8 cm) long. Approximately 17,000 of these tiny toads used to live at the Kihansi Gorge in Tanzania.

Spray from waterfalls once kept the land there moist. This made a perfect habitat for the Kihansi spray toad. But in 2001, a dam was built to help provide electricity. The dam held back most of the water that had flowed over the falls. There wasn't enough to create a spray. The land quickly dried up. In 2009, these toads were declared extinct in the wild.

Luckily, scientists saw the danger ahead of time. In 1999, zoo workers

RESCUE MISSION

US zookeepers visited the gorge in 1999 to collect Kihansi spray toads before the dam construction started. They put them in plastic bags with moss and then into coolers. The toads went to six US zoos. Zookeepers quickly had to figure out what water, light, and food the toads needed. Toads at four of the zoos did not survive. But New York's Bronx Zoo and Ohio's Toledo Zoo succeeded. A Toledo zookeeper figured out that a halogen bulb provided the best light. A zookeeper in the Bronx made a safe food supply by breeding fruit flies and weevils.

The tiny Kihansi toads were first discovered in 1996.

collected 499 toads. They planned to breed the toads and put them back into the wild once their habitat was restored. A sprinkler system was installed at the gorge to keep the ground moist in the same way the waterfall had. The company that operates the dam makes sure the sprinkler system is working. While this system was being set up, zoos were able to breed more than 2,000 Kihansi spray toads. Scientists started releasing them back to their home in 2012. If the toads thrive in their new habitat, their status will be upgraded from extinct in the wild to critically endangered.

5
Size in acres (2 ha) of the Kihansi spray toad's entire home habitat.

Status: Extinct in the wild
Population:
   Approximately 2,000
Home: Tanzania
Life Span: Five years

6

SAGALLA CAECILIAN ON THE REBOUND UNDERGROUND

The Sagalla caecilian has a long, thin body like an earthworm. But unlike an earthworm, it has a mouth, tentacles, and nostrils. It uses its tentacles to find food, such as earthworms, termites, and other insects living in the soil. The Sagalla caecilian mostly lives underground in an area of just 18 square miles (46.6 sq km) in Kenya. That's about half the size of Manhattan.

The habitat used to be covered in forest. Over the years, this area has changed.

Pesticides and chemicals used in farming polluted the soil. Trees and other plants were cut down, and the soil washed away. Eucalyptus trees were planted, but these trees make the soil hard and dry. The Sagalla caecilians need rich, damp

Sagalla caecilians live only on Sagalla Hill in Kenya.

The Sagalla caecilian uses its nose and its tentacles to find prey.

soil like that of a forest. The water in the soil keeps their skin moist. It also provides a good habitat for their prey.

The species was listed as critically endangered in 2006.

Conservationists have been working to restore the habitat. They removed the eucalyptus trees and replanted other plants and trees. As of 2013, the Sagalla caecilians' status was no longer listed as critical.

THINK ABOUT IT

The Sagalla caecilian was first discovered in 2005. Scientists have not studied it much yet. If you were a scientist studying it, what would you like to find out?

12
Approximate length in inches (30 cm) of a Sagalla caecilian.

Status: Endangered
Population: Unknown
Home: Kenya
Life Span: Unknown

BIG EFFORTS TO SAVE GIANT CHINESE SALAMANDER

Giant Chinese salamanders are the largest amphibians in the world. They can grow up to five feet (1.5 m) long and weigh more than 50 pounds (22.7 kg). These giants live in cool mountain streams and

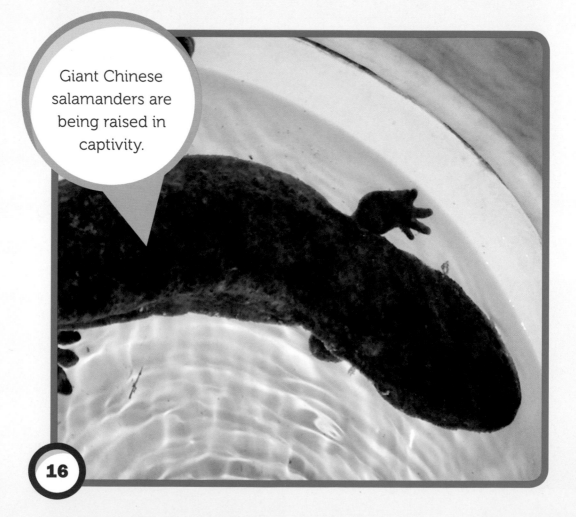

Giant Chinese salamanders are being raised in captivity.

60

Percent of body length that is the salamander's tail.

Status: Critically endangered
Population: Unknown
Home: China
Life Span: 50 years

lakes. The population has decreased by 80 percent since the 1960s. But conservationists are working hard on a turnaround.

The biggest threat comes from people. The salamanders are easy to catch. A hunter can sell a salamander for approximately $50 per pound (0.5 kg). The meat is expensive, but some people enjoy it as a treat. People also use parts of this salamander to make medicines.

Now more farmers are raising the salamanders, too. Farms have to be licensed to raise them. To get a license, farmers have to release a percentage of the salamanders they raise back into the wild. Conservationists are also working on plans for breeding centers in China.

In the wild, giant Chinese salamanders' natural habitat has been declining. Dams have turned streams into standing water or dried-up ditches. Where the water still flows, mining and farming have polluted it. China has set aside land with clear streams as nature preserves so that the salamanders have a place to thrive. The number of salamanders living on the preserves is growing.

STARTING SMALL

Male giant Chinese salamanders are protective fathers. After mating, the female lays approximately 500 eggs in an underwater burrow. The female then leaves, but the male stays to protect the eggs from predators. After approximately two months, the eggs hatch. The larvae start out approximately one inch (2.5 cm) long.

17

RANCHERS STEP UP TO SAVE CHIRICAHUA LEOPARD FROGS

When Chiricahua leopard frogs call to one another, it sounds like snoring. Males make this call when they are looking for a mate. Females lay egg sacs during the summer. Each sac contains more than 1,000 eggs. Tadpoles hatch from the eggs and take three to nine months to grow into frogs. But for all this to take place, the tadpoles need constant sources of standing water. Those have become harder to find.

WORLD INVADERS

Bullfrogs used to live only in eastern North America. In the late 1800s, people brought the bullfrogs to California. They wanted to raise the frogs to eat their legs. Bullfrogs were also taken to other countries. Bullfrog populations grew in places they had never been before. They didn't have many predators in the new locations. The bullfrogs became the predators, eating smaller animals, such as the Chiricahua leopard frog tadpoles.

Chiricahua leopard frogs need lots of water to survive.

Chiricahua leopard frogs feed on insects and freshwater shrimp.

Chiricahua leopard frogs live in Arizona and New Mexico. But construction, dams, and cattle ranches have drained away the natural wetlands and springs there. In some of the Chiricahua leopard frogs' habitats, people introduced new predators, such as bullfrogs and crayfish. These animals started eating leopard frog eggs, tadpoles, and adults.

The frogs used to live in more than 400 locations in the Southwest United States. But that number fell to 80 by the 1990s. After the frogs were listed as threatened in 2002, some ranchers decided to help. They built or restored water tanks, wells, and concrete ponds on their land to create new water sources. Then they rescued tadpoles from areas that were drying up and put them in the new habitats.

More frogs were bred in captivity. Other landowners stepped in to help. They worked with officials to release the leopard frogs into the wild. By 2010, 10,000 frogs were set free in their new habitats.

6,000
Number of eggs a female lays in one season.

Status: Vulnerable
Population: More than 10,000
Home: Arizona and New Mexico
Life Span: 18 years

NEW EFFORTS HELP WYOMING TOADS

Wyoming toads have poor eyesight. They have to wait for their prey to move to find it. They eat ants, beetles, and other insects. The toads' prey used to be plentiful in the Laramie Basin, where they live. Then people sprayed pesticides to get rid of mosquitoes. The toads had less to eat. Disease and habitat loss also may have affected them. The Wyoming toads were listed as an endangered species in 1984. But by that point, some feared they were already extinct.

Then in 1987, a small population of Wyoming toads was discovered in a lake. The area was turned into a nature reserve. Conservationists started managing the habitat to make sure the toads would thrive. Wyoming toads need warm water to mate. Cattle used to graze on the prairies, keeping the grass short. Without shade from tall grasses,

SETTING FIRES FOR WILDLIFE

The prairies in the Laramie Basin are burned approximately every four years when the toads are hibernating. Before the fires are set, workers walk through to move other animals out. The animals go into burrows or fly or run away. A fire can improve the habitat for many animals. It stops trees and brush from growing. These can crowd out the animals and other plants. It also helps new grass to start growing. Many animals use the grass for nests or hiding.

3–20

Days it takes for eggs to hatch into tadpoles.

Status: Extinct in the wild
Population: Unknown
Home: Wyoming
Life Span: 8–10 years

In 2012, conservationists used fire to stop the plants from growing too high. Zoo workers have been raising more tadpoles and toads in captivity. They have released more than 160,000 into their new habitat. Wyoming toads will continue to be listed as extinct in the wild until scientists see if these new populations survive.

the sun would heat up the shallow water. Conservationists brought back cattle to eat the grass. This way the toads would have more breeding places.

Individual Wyoming toads can be identified by their warts and other markings.

WATER LIMITS HELP TEXAS BLIND SALAMANDER

The Texas blind salamander cannot see. Its eyes look like two tiny black dots under its skin. But the salamander doesn't need vision to survive. It lives underwater in complete darkness in underground caves.

The water in the caves comes from the Edwards Aquifer in San Marcos, Texas, near San Antonio. The aquifer also supplies water to the people of the city. A lot of water is needed for washing clothes, watering lawns, and flushing toilets. Too much was being used. There wasn't enough left for the salamanders.

When people realized this, the Texas legislature set limits on how much water people could use. To save water, some people bought new toilets. Older toilets used approximately six gallons (22.7 L) of water per flush. New models only used one gallon (3.8 L). These water-saving ideas have helped save the salamander. These salamanders are difficult to count because they live in underground caves. But some of the Texas blind salamanders flow out through a pipe at the aquifer. Scientists track these to get an idea of how the population down below is doing. Since water usage has decreased, the number of salamanders has increased.

THINK ABOUT IT

Imagine you live near the aquifer. How would you feel about water limits? Write a letter to the local newspaper to explain your position.

Blind salamanders' skin has almost no color. It looks pink because of the blood vessels underneath showing through.

4
Number of toes on each front foot.

Status: Vulnerable
Population: Unknown
Home: San Marcos, Texas
Life Span: 70 years

HABITATS RESTORED FOR WHITE-BELLIED FROGS

In swampy areas of Australia, water used to come up through the ground. White-bellied frogs would lay eggs in the puddles that formed. The tadpoles would grow in the puddles, too.

White-bellied frogs are about the same size as the end of a person's thumb.

HOME SWEET HOME

During mating season, the male white-bellied frog finds a low, wet area. Then he calls for a female. She lays her eggs in the same place. The eggs are in a jelly-like substance. Tadpoles grow inside the eggs and hatch as tadpoles. They stay in the puddle until they are grown.

Then the frogs' habitat changed. Trees were cut down to make room for cattle. Dams were built to provide water for crops. The land dried up, and the puddles were gone. The frogs began to disappear, too.

People began working to protect the habitat. Land was set aside for the frogs and other wildlife. Fences were built to keep them safe from the cattle. But predators still ate the white-bellied frogs' eggs and tadpoles.

In 2008, Perth Zoo workers started collecting egg clusters and raising them in captivity. When they grow into frogs, the workers put them back in the wild. From 2010 to 2013, more than 200 frogs were released.

50
Number of white-bellied frog populations in Australia.

Status: Critically endangered
Population: Approximately 3,000
Home: Australia
Life Span: Approximately 16 years

MOUNTAIN YELLOW-LEGGED FROGS ESCAPE A PREDATOR

Mountain yellow-legged frogs live high up in the Sierra Nevada Mountains. They are one of the few amphibians to thrive in the cold, snowy winters there. During the fall and winter, the frogs dive into deep pools to hibernate. At the bottom, the water is very cold but doesn't freeze. The frogs' skin takes in small amounts of oxygen from the water. When the snow melts, they come back to the surface to lay eggs. In warmer months, tourists used to be able to see these frogs all around the lakes and streams. Then the frogs began to disappear.

Mountain yellow-legged frogs move in bursts of two to five hops before stopping to rest.

When they're not in the water, mountain yellow-legged frogs bask in sunny spots.

One reason was a change in their habitat. From the 1920s to 1990s, California state workers added trout to many lakes. They hoped more people would visit the lakes to go fishing. But the efforts had an unexpected effect. The trout ate the frog eggs and young frogs. They also ate a lot of insects, so the frogs had less to eat. The mountain yellow-legged frogs began to die out.

In 2001, state workers began catching the trout and taking them out of the lakes. By 2011, they had removed almost 44,000 fish from 19 lakes. In three of the lakes, the number of frogs in the wild grew

from 190 to more than 18,000 in the first three years. Since then, their numbers have ranged from 3,600 to more than 11,000.

2–4
Years it takes for a tadpole to grow into a young frog.

Status: Endangered
Population: Varies; thousands in monitored lakes
Home: Sierra Nevada Mountains
Life Span: 12–16 years

27

FACT SHEET

- The word *amphibian* means "both lives." Many amphibians spend part of their life in water and part of their life on land. Amphibians include frogs, toads, salamanders, newts, and caecilians.

- There are approximately 5,800 species of frogs and toads, approximately 580 species of salamanders and newts, and approximately 170 species of caecilians. Scientists estimate that one-third or more of all amphibians are in danger of becoming extinct.

- Scientists have discovered that chemicals from some amphibians' skin have uses in medicine. Some can be used to treat pain or to fight infections.

- Amphibians are important parts of many food chains. Many amphibians eat insects and other smaller creatures. They are also a food source for some larger animals. When they disappear from a habitat, insect populations such as mosquitoes often grow. And larger animals lose a food source.

- Amphibians are a good indicator of the health of a habitat. Their close relationship with water causes them to show changes when water conditions change. If the water is polluted, amphibians start to die off. Water pollution can affect other animals in a habitat and people, as well.

- The main threats amphibians face are pollution, habitat loss, disease, and invasive species. In recent years, many amphibian species have been infected with a deadly fungus called Chytrid. The fungus damages the skin. Amphibians need their skin to drink and absorb certain nutrients. Once a species is infected with Chytrid, people have to act quickly to rescue its members. Scientists are still trying to find a solution to the spread of Chytrid in the wild.

- Many countries have laws protecting endangered animals. In 1973, the US Congress passed the Endangered Species Act. It requires state and federal government agencies to monitor and protect species that might become extinct. It also bans people from hunting, catching, trading, or possessing animals and plants that are protected.

GLOSSARY

aquifer
A water-bearing layer of rock underground.

breed
To produce offspring.

conservationist
A person who tries to protect natural resources.

drought
A long period of dry weather.

endangered
Threatened with extinction.

extinct
The death of all members of a species.

habitat
The place where an animal naturally lives and grows.

larvae
A very young form of a species that looks like a tiny worm.

pesticide
A substance that is used to destroy pests, such as insects.

polluted
Containing man-made waste.

predator
An animal that kills or eats another animal.

prey
An animal that is killed or eaten by another animal.

species
A group of animals or plants that are similar and can produce young.

threatened
To be in danger of becoming extinct.

FOR MORE INFORMATION

Books

Berger, Gilda, and Melvin Berger. *True or False: Amphibians.* New York: Scholastic, 2011.

Goldish, Meish. *Slimy Salamanders.* New York: Bearport Publishing, 2010.

Housel, Debra. *Slithering Reptiles and Amphibians.* Huntington Beach, CA: Teacher Created Materials, 2013.

Ransom, Candice. *Endangered and Extinct Amphibians.* Minneapolis, MN: Lerner, 2014.

Spelman, Lucy. *National Geographic Animal Encyclopedia.* Washington, DC: National Geographic Children's Books, 2012.

Websites

Kids Discover Spotlight: Amphibians
www.kidsdiscover.com/spotlight/about-amphibians

National Geographic Kids: Animals and Pets
kids.nationalgeographic.com/kids/animals

San Diego Zoo Kids: Amphibians
kids.sandiegozoo.org/animals/amphibians

INDEX

About the Author

Samantha Bell is a graduate of Furman University and has taught writing and art to both children and adults. She has written or illustrated more than 20 books for children.

READ MORE FROM 12-STORY LIBRARY

Every 12-Story Library book is available in many formats, including Amazon Kindle and Apple iBooks. For more information, visit your device's store or 12StoryLibrary.com.